Through The Eyes Of A Flower

WRITTEN BY

KELLY GLOVER

COVER ART BY

JONATHAN VIZCUÑA

CONTENTS

Crushed Petals

Women are silent flowers
Prettiest when quiet
We do not wilt
When they crush our petals
Strip our leaves

Divine feminine roots
Remain and regenerate
Exquisite thorns sharpen

We are walking targets
With bullseye breasts
Shot with shame
From the moment of fertility

The blood of life
Natural as breath
Still taboo table talk

Be a beauty, wear lipstick
Just not that particular shade
Of sunburnt whore

Look nice, paint your nails
But not the same dark red
That will stain his sheets
When he's had his way with you

Why don't we report our rapes?
Our assaults?
Our complaints?
Flowers don't speak
When bees steal their pollen

As the last blooms are spent
A new season buds
We are flooded
Drowning in courage and confidence

Petals look best in a bouquet
The more we gather
The more beautiful we become
Holding each other up
By our weakest stems

The blooms are getting louder
As the shame falls away
The roses have found their voices
Briars surround our choices

wonder

I wonder when I learned to swim
Sideways in depression's ocean current
Rather than gurgle the salty waves
I wonder if you can still feel the energy
That I throw into the universe
Even when you close your world to me
I wonder if I can write you
Out of my existence
Put the period on our sentence
I wonder why I lay myself bare
Only to be rejected
By those that never even try to deserve me
I wonder if the ghosts of a past me
Will ever stop haunting my present
Or holding me back from my future
I wonder why I over analyze
Every mundane human detail
With my command of the language
No wonder I am so inundated
With all things rhetorical
I am simply nothing short of
Absolutely wonderful

It Never Was

Did you forget my name yet
Gorgeous
It never was

I was just a sequin eyed
Prize
A silky white pair of
Thighs
Used to drain your
Insecurities
Mix them with my
Impurities

I always like the way
My name sounds better
Through the lips of a lying mouth
Your mirror is shattered
I caught a glimpse of myself
In the shards
And I have never looked so
Foolish

Let the other many beautiful
Reflections
Make you feel alive
Because my name is
Drop dead
Gorgeous
It never was

Balance Her

Heel in front of toe
She teeters on her
Line of balance
The left side boils
While the right simmers
As she glides between
The loves of her life
Each one pulling
At her fingertips
Trying to disrupt
Her equilibrium
She will crouch
Sway and bend
But never fall
Her mistakes
Are just clouds
She rides to
The new destination
Her next gymnast
Routine

With My Love

I want to be the coffee in that morning mug
Your mouth so eager for its first sip
That you don't mind when I scorch your throat
With my love

The bubbling cheese on the pizza
That melts the roof of your mouth
Your pleasure ruined at first bite
With my love

Everyone knows we remember pain
Much quicker than we do the pleasure
I never kill softly, only slaughter
With my love

Colorless

The blue has dripped from the sky

Rained us out

Colorless

The amount of loss not proportionate

To our short moments together

Hospital room pain scales

Show a smiling face

Morphing into agony

One through ten

How bad does it hurt?

If there are love scales

Ours have started to tip

A starry eyed lover turns to tears

Medicate accordingly

I thought you were the whole ocean

But you were just a creek

That wet my socks

My color is bleeding through again

Deep violet ruby

Something you could never dream

Disposable

Disposable woman

In all her domestic misery

Left behind

Like the watermelon rind

Once her blades are rusted

The knives no longer sharp

She finds herself in the dumpster

With the rest of the discarded decisions

Everyone is replaceable

I will remove myself

Before you can discard me

Never bothering to erase you

I am the same

With or without your desire

The Mother Theresa of deviant souls

Shakes the dark angel from her back

As he slinks away

To find his next prey

He'll realize the writer

Has penned his end

These words could be about

Any mistake I've ever misplaced

But I bet you think they're about you

Disposable man

Garbage

She is the type of girl
Everyone admires
But no one
Will hold her hand
She will read you stories
From her rare heart
But no one
Speaks her language
They want to fuck her
But never sleep with her
She is easily disposable
The most unique
Piece of garbage
You have ever seen

Garden Stroll

Come to my garden

There is plenty to see and say

If your spirit is hard

The weeds will scare you away

Ferocious flowers

All the colors of gloom

Glistening dew showers

Come when it's time to bloom

Vicious violets

Rancid roses

Seeping silent

Petal poses

Swallow your pride

Get drunk off that pain

The only way inside

Is to splash down the drain

Be bitten by a snake

Stung by a bee

Just don't make the mistake

Of missing shade from my trees

Fragrance eviscerates the senses

Burning of paradise

Break down my fences

Breeze through more than twice

Violent Purple

Muscle memory
Makes me wonder
Love is like death
At some point
It will become
Violent purple
Never meant
For permanence
As temporary
As my hair color
I need to create
Enough stories
Without you in them
That I don't know
Who belongs where
I just wish
The lonely
Would leave me alone

Jealousy

Jealousy is my angry little sister
That bites when she feels threatened
Her eyes glow brighter
Fluorescent fangs of emerald
That drip disenchantment
She asks all the questions
That don't demand answers
I've learned to hold her hand
Let her have her moment
Be seen and felt
She is nothing but love
Misrepresented

Pie

Christmas trees and jack-o-lanterns
Treasured for a month
Tossed to the sidewalk to decay
Planted, tendered, and harvested
Trucked out of forests and gardens
Solely for our baubles
And aesthetic pleasure

What happens
To the evergreens and gourds
That nobody buys
Cut and left to die
The ones that don't get chosen
By red cheeked children
With magic in their eyes

I belong where they do
Abandoned, discarded, and forgotten
Left for mulch

Like the remnants of a pumpkin patch
The day after Halloween
The only thing they are still good for
Is pumpkin pie
Someone's dessert
The best I could be is pie

Toxicity

Toxic femininity
Wants me to soften
Drip melted butter
That adapts to the cracks
In the crust
Of the bread of life

Toxic positivity
Prefers I live a lie
Disregard and disown
My natural darkness
Eat my road rage
And ask for another

Toxic masculinity
Tells me boys will be boys
Emotionally void
Violently entitled
To my body and self value
Above all else

An alpha female is a diamond
But that's not the real treasure
It's the multicolored stones inside
That can detoxify
Neutralize toxicity
With my divine femininity

Mother Alone

Single mother lover
Left on her own
Because instinctively he knew
She wouldn't try to find another

Her children the one priority
There is no time
For dating games
Her kids the only royalty

Single forever person
To protect her offspring
From the heartache
Of another man's desertion

For the woman she is
Appreciate her
Then leave her alone
To raise her kids

Beautiful Disease

Tragic tastes like love on my lips

I am the hot side of the pillow

Flip me to find your comfort

Sexual transmission

A beautiful disease

No course of antibiotics can cure

You can try to detox

But you will never sweat me

Out of your system

Discard me like a peanut's remnant

You'll end up cutting your foot

On the misplaced shell

I will creep through your immune system

Wreak havoc on your dopamine

Devour your energy and feed my own

With the remains

Until all you are left with

Is an incoherent whisper

Of what could have been

Bloom

When the rest of the world
Needs to feed on your petals
All I want are the scratches
Draw blood with your thorns
Let the breeze know
When you're ready to bloom

Smokey

I was just a single cigarette
Of your chain smoking habit
But I don't biodegrade
When you are ready to quit
I can be your nicotine patch
Rip me off and throw me away
After you have been cured

Clear Eyes

Every problem I've ever had
Started with a brown eyed man
You can never pull the truth
From those dark pools
Faking intimacy
Is worse than cheating
A lie is a lie all the way around
Even if the truth will never be found
When you believe your own lies
There is no way for me to win
Brown eyed doll man
I'll stop forcing my love on you
The passion must have somewhere to go
So this rage poetry stews
While I forcefully fall
Face first out of love
I hope I haunt you
You were just the scrimmage
The real game is rain delayed
From now on I'll look for eyes like mine
Ones that are see through
And much prettier when they cry

Drink

I pour my heart into you
Only for it to be gulped down
And pissed away
May it leave you
With kidney stones

Black Stag

Beautiful black stag
Hunted for his vigor
The treasure is his head
Mounted over the bed
For sport we celebrate his death

A solo king of the beasts
He loses his magnificence
If his head is trapped and taken away
Not every hunter wants him in this way
A doe knows a stag must play

But just like there are many worthy hunters
The stag is not so alone
There are wild boar and ravens in the race
A white fox and dire wolves to chase
A haunted huntress always finds her prey

Marbled

Traveling down
The staircase
Of my mind
I don't hold
Onto handrails
But prefer
To step directly
On all the marbles
Placed sporadically
On the risers
It may hurt
On the way down
But at least I know
I have been somewhere

Devour

To the man that just wants
To devour the essence
Of any goddess
That crosses his path
Feast
Make her your snack
Just realize
For your last meal
Dessert
Is your own skin
So you better
Like the taste
Of what will be
On your plate

Sidewalk Flower

Expire me

Cover me with your distaste

There is no fear in fierce

Making it easy to stomp away

Each step drives more steel into my heart

Like a rusty nail delivering tetanus

To a naked appendage

I intimidate men

I am no timid date

Domination is the story

Intimidation wrote the book

I am the quick breath in between the rhymes

Of a rockstar's ballad

A solo verse of brutal truth

Like a flower growing in a sidewalk crack

Radiating through the cement

Waiting patiently for what

Nature rains down upon me

And the heel of a boot to stamp me out

Marinate

She marinates in the mud
Searching the sediment
For gems worth gathering
Even dirt will sparkle
With the right ray of light
Depression ate the manic
Morose beauty
But it is never enough
To satisfy a simmering gut
There is beauty in beasts
A blaze for every night
She no longer looks for heroes
Her superpowers are enough
Scintillation
All on their own

Shit Shower

Don't piss on me and call it a bath
Or shit on me and call it moisturizer
I've been in that shower before
My ever present soap
Will wash you down the drain

Divine Intervention

Lately disappointment
Has become my favorite flavor
It tastes like missed opportunities
And unused lingerie
Every time I try
To climb your tree
You knock me down again
The ground is soft
But my fingers bleed
From clawing at your bark
I wait for some grand gesture
A profession of adoration
That will never come
I must be my own
Divine intervention

Butterfly Guts

Those manufactured butterflies
You put in my stomach
Aren't special
If you place
Fluttering cocoons
Everywhere you go
Like a child on Christmas
Your eyes are wide with
The next shiny package
Before you have unwrapped
The gift you already have
Naked in your hands
I am the one you want to lie to
The one you want to leave
The hell I've been through
Warmed me and now
I search for flames of relief
When my residual heat
Becomes just a repeat
And my blaze
Begins to freeze
You'll know this spider
Digested your butterflies
In her guts of fire

Bread

Men are bread
They fill you up
To leave you malnourished
Naughty carbohydrates
Break you down
Into a glucose high
Only to send you crashing
When all the sugar is spent
Buttery biscuits
With a never ending need
To rise
Some are plain white
Some are toasted wheat
Some will leave sesame seeds
Lodged in your teeth
I'm ready to be
Gluten free
Find some other meat
To fill your sandwich
Your crumbs
No longer sustain

Roots

There is something below rock bottom

Roots

Burrow deep beneath

Excavate

Lie dormant

Seek nourishment from down under

Nurture a new beginning

From a rock bottom ending

Fleeting scenery upon the descent

Ragged edged stones to break the fall

Blood spills

Giving birth to seeds of enlightenment

Roots spread wide

Quenched in tears from the well

Below rock bottom

Regrowth

Seasons cycle

Branches crack from the weight

Of years undertaken

The pressure of those to come

Forcing upward that rock bottom

Even death can not destroy

Roots remain stagnant

Decomposing worm lunch

After all the scavengers have fed

The bird of prey

Devours what remains

Feeds its children

With the essence of those roots

Defecation sprouts

Rejuvenated spirits

A landslide disrupts

Leaving different jagged edges

For a new generation

To perpetuate a legacy of the roots

Found under rock bottom

Muse

You never existed
I carved out
Of my desires
All the qualities
I look for in a man
Placed them inside
Your sculpted body
A vessel for my artistry
Looked better in the mind
Than on my paper
Your muses are many
Mine solo
Once I decide love
Was only myself
In disguise all along
You will be the one
Searching for me
In every female you see

Notch

Practice
Makes
Perfect
But the
Fox
Is a
Hound
Every
Animal
A lesson
Another
Notch
Lives
Forever
On the
Bedpost
Of never
Was
Or will
Be

Rejection
The knife
That digs
The grooves
Lost
Boys
Red
Flags
Have
The
Sharpest
Lines

Chip off The old Heart

The bleeding heart on my sleeve
Takes issue
With the sharp chip on my shoulder
There isn't enough space
To wear both at once
So I tuck tight
Whichever one gets in the way
At any given moment
What you ask of me
Is what you will receive
My love or my disdain
No in between
My heart can beat so loud
Nothing else will be heard
But that chip will choke you
Without saying a word

Black Ankle Socks

Overdrafts and fraudulent charges
Dull razors in cold showers
Bad internet connections
Broken box spring with no mattress
Ingrown toenails and paper cuts
The heel of a loaf of bread
To make a burnt grilled cheese
Black ankle socks with white shoes
These are things I'd rather have and do
Than spend another thought on you

Toilet Flower

Even God herself
Probably got herself
Into some muddy water
Do not look
For professionals
To turn your
Lucifer
Loose if your
Heart beats
Outside it's chest
Hurl yourself
Into that sea
With all the rest
Of the lonely fish
Before he guts you
Throws you back
Like a toilet flower
You'll grow
More vibrant
With every
Piece of shit
That flows through
All your deepest cracks

Tethered and Tangled

Humans are
Just wind chimes
With tethered
Connections
We all crave
Each air gust
Tinkles
Dangling strings
As we bump
Into each other
Become twisted
During the storms
Tangled for years
Just to be cut short
The wind will always
Push you into others
A mosaic of
Music while it blows

Rottweiler

She just wants
To share herself
With someone
But no one wants
To rot while her
Thoughts straighten out
Rottweiler
No bone can satisfy
She gives herself
Heat lightning
Flashes of possibilities
Ways to make them
Remember
Her presence
Lick their wounds
By digging deeper
Her own scars
Every member
Of the team
Her presents
Fantom limbs
Of the rejection
She thrives on

Twisted Tree

There is nothing else to conquer
When you are your own mountain
My emotions poison potions
Pulsating waves through my ocean
Don't beat around my burning bush
The briars aren't forgiving and
The flowers aren't worth your trouble
I am a twisted tree
In a solitary forest
Robust gnarly
Full of fungus
Unassailable at all times

Festering

When you manifest
What a man is festering
His sores become yours
A life of soaring by yourself
Is what's best to manifest

Intimacy without Expectations

The highest form of respect and admiration we can give to another human being is intimacy without expectations. Tracing the inside of what makes a person tick with the gentlest of intentions. Compassion need not cum with passion. Licking another person's wounds does not have to deepen my own. To create a safe space for another human to be seen and heard is a powerful way to be remembered. As I dine on my personal pain, I can chew it up and serve it to others that can't yet swallow or don't yet have the teeth to cut their own. Let the beauty continue to overtake the beast.

Two Lips

A tulip looks completely different
When it's petals are pried open
Like any woman when her two lips
Are forcefully parted
We change
Become more enchanting
When too, lips that have been silent
Now refuse to stay quiet

Bonus

I don't need you
To tell me
You love me
I'm satisfied
Just being
Your memory
Think of me
When you see
The color purple
Not Prince
Or that movie
More like
The hue
Of that bruise
On your shin
When you bang
It on the same
Coffee table
For the fortieth time
That's me
The hummingbird
At your feeder
Here and gone
Before you can blink
A strobe light
Flashing glimpses
Of me
When you remember
I will know
That will be enough

An extra special note of appreciation
to one of my favorite human beings.
Time stopped when you forgot your
watch and I still catch myself swaying
to your memory. You know who you
are. You know which words are here for
you. I hope you think they are beautiful.
Thank you endlessly for the gentle
inspiration, encouragement and
for allowing me to just be myself.
You don't even know what you did.

Kelly Glover is a single mother from
Greensboro, North Carolina with an out
of the ordinary love for flowers and words.
when she's not growing poetry or children,
you can find her in the garden making a floral
wonderland. Her poems, prose,
and short stories can be found in
several literary journals and international
anthologies. Follow her thoughts on
Instagram@serenitysavagewritespowitry.

Jonathan Vizcuña is a visual artist and
senior web designer from Caracas,
venezuela. Spreading art everywhere he
goes, his unique papercraft sculptures have
been featured in such places as Miami art
week and Piedmont International airport.
This multi talented man also knows how
to stir up a crowd with his euphoric high
energy musical mixes. You can find his
work at Jonathanvizcuna.com and
@vizcunaart on Instagram.

www.ingramcontent.com/pod-product-compliance
Lightning Source LLC
Chambersburg PA
CBHW060508160726
47992CB00003B/1383